RAILWAY JACK

THE TRUE STORY OF AN AMAZING BABOON

WRITTEN BY KT JOHNSTON
ILLUSTRATED BY César Samaniego

CAPSTONE EDITIONS
a capstone imprint

Rrrrrr! A train rumbled into Uitenhage Station at the tip of South Africa. Opened in 1875, the charming station was nearly brand new. The train squealed to a stop and exhaled a *whooooosh* of steam. While people bustled on and off, a railway guard named Jim Wide walked from engine to caboose. Jim ducked underneath and looked in between the cars. He inspected each one to make sure the train was safe.

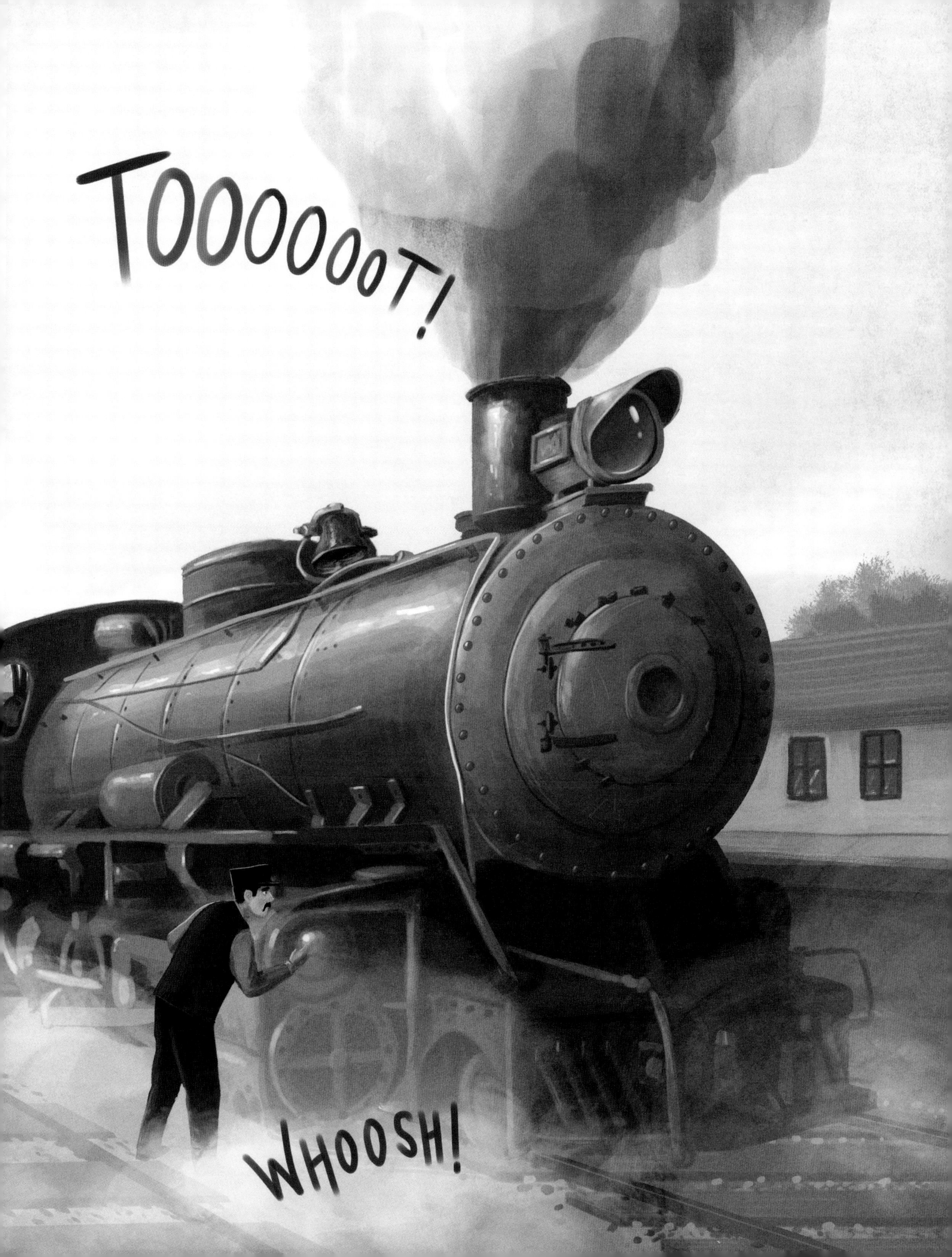
TOOOOOOT!
WHOOSH!

One day Jim had an accident when he was helping with track repairs. His legs were damaged badly. Doctors were not able to fix them, so they amputated Jim's legs below the knee. Jim couldn't inspect trains anymore.

Jim needed to find a way to get around and to get back to work. He made himself wooden legs. He was able to walk with them, using a cane for balance. He sent a telegram to the railway authorities begging to be rehired.

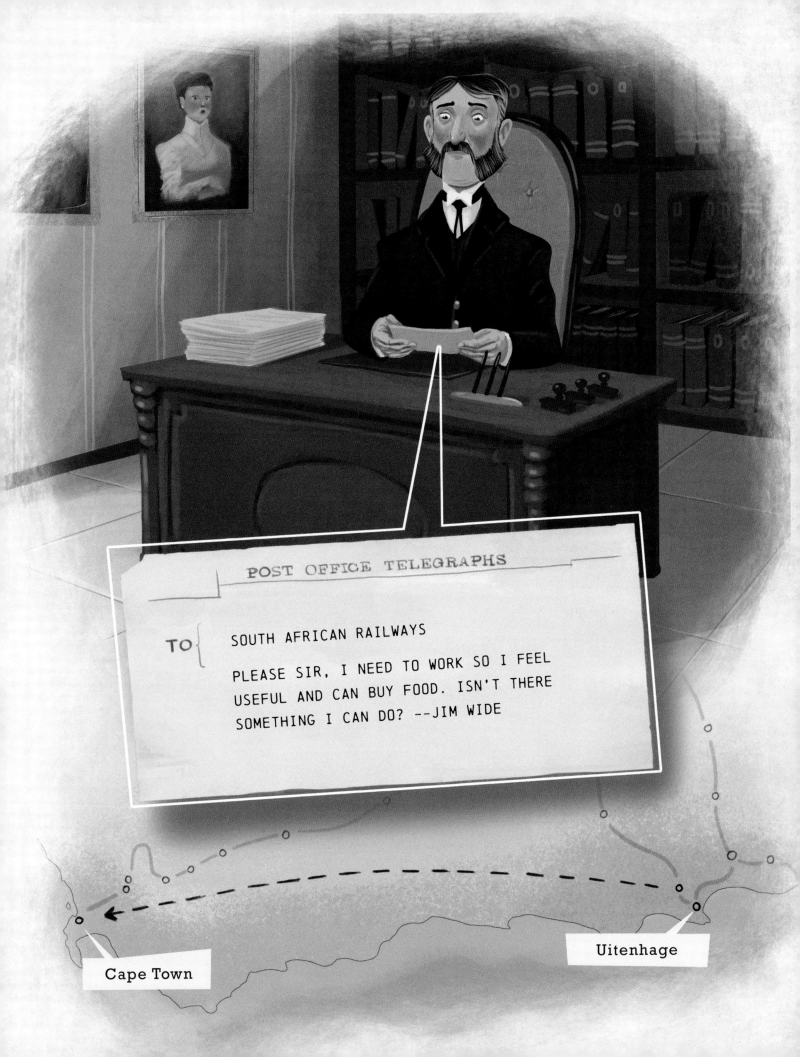

Uitenhage
Station

coal yard

signal hut

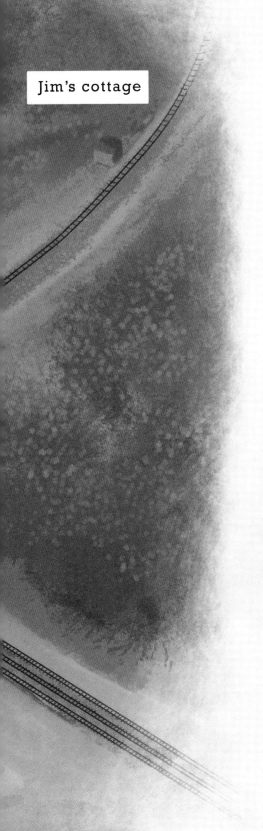

Jim's cottage

The authorities wanted to help Jim, so they gave him a new job as a signalman at Uitenhage Station. As a signalman, Jim helped trains move to the proper tracks for their destinations. He did this by pulling levers that stood in a row outside his post, a signal hut located in the rail yard. Long cables connected the levers to switch points on the tracks. When a lever was pulled, the cable moved the rails. This switched the train to a different track.

Jim was also responsible for inspecting the switch points. But some of them were difficult to get to on his wooden legs. For this, Jim built a cart to sit on. It had a hand crank to make it go and special wheels that rolled on the tracks. Now Jim could do his work and also ride the tracks to work from his cottage just up the line.

But even with wooden legs and a cart, Jim struggled to do some tasks. He was always on the lookout for other clever solutions.

One afternoon at the market, Jim saw a young baboon assisting a man.

"That's right, Jack! Lead the oxen," Jim heard the man say to the baboon.

"Sir?" Jim said. "That monkey looks so smart! I wonder if he could learn things that would help me. Is he for sale?"

The man listened to Jim's story. He realized Jack could be a great help to Jim. They struck a deal, and Jim had himself a baboon.

To Jim's delight, he found that the baboon learned quickly and was very careful about his work. Jack paid close attention and tried to do things just the way Jim did them. Jack never needed to be told twice.

Jack could tell when he'd done things right. Jim would pat him tenderly and say, "Good boy, Jack!" Jack responded with even greater efforts to please Jim.

Jack even helped Jim grow their food. The vegetable garden took a lot of water. Jack would eagerly work the pump handle—*up-down-up-down-fast-fast-fast!*—and then he would drop to the ground to catch his breath. Before long he'd pop up and go at it again!

People thought it was funny to see a baboon working so hard. Jim also found Jack entertaining, but mostly he was grateful. He knew Jack made the effort for him.

Jim also taught Jack how to put his cart on the tracks. Jack would roll the cart from the cottage to the rail. Then, making sure his tail was not in the way, he'd sit back on his haunches and hoist the front wheels over the first rail. He'd give the whole thing a twist, and all four wheels would settle onto the rails with a clatter. Jack was so strong that he made it look easy!

Jim no longer had to wear himself out using the hand crank. Jack could push the cart to and from work. While Jim took his seat, Jack would carefully lock the cottage door as Jim had taught him to do. Then Jack would give the key to Jim, and off they'd go. Using his feet, Jack gripped the tracks step by step as he pushed the cart along, working hard on the uphill slopes . . .

. . . then hopping onto the cart with Jim for a fun ride down the other side!

"Hoo hoo hoo!" hooted Jack.

"Ha ha, Jack! You silly baboon!" laughed Jim.

Jack screeched in reply. Jim knew this meant that Jack found himself funny as well.

Some of the things that Jim struggled with were fun
challenges for Jack. He enjoyed learning new things. He
was so helpful that Jim came to think of Jack not merely
as his assistant but also as his best friend. It was clear
Jack felt the same way. He would sit with his arm around
Jim's neck and stroke Jim's hand, chattering endlessly.

Jim fed Jack and took care of him in the ways known to a human. And Jack took care of Jim in the ways known to a baboon. He was a good night watchman. Nobody could get near the cottage unannounced! And when Jim got teased, Jack stood up for him. One time Jack hooted and flapped a dirty coal sack at a bully. The frightened man fled in a cloud of black dust!

At the rail yard, Jack watched Jim work. When a train blasted its whistle four times, it meant the engineer needed the key for the coal yard. The engine burned coal to create steam to power the train.

Toot toot toot toot!

Jim reached into the signal hut and took the key off its nail. He hobbled across the rough ground to hand it to the engineer as the train slowly chugged past. When the engineer finished loading, he returned the key, and Jim put it back in the hut.

Toot Toot Toot Toot!

Before long, Jack knew what to do when he heard four whistles. One day, without a word from Jim, Jack dashed to the hut and snatched the key. He hurried to the tracks and held it up for the engineer. When the job was finished, Jack put the key back on its nail.

"Well, well, Jack, you smart baboon!" Jim said, surprised.

"Hoo hoo hoo!" Jack replied.

From that day on, it was Jack who provided the coal yard key when four whistles sounded. Jack became Jim's helper at work as well as at home.

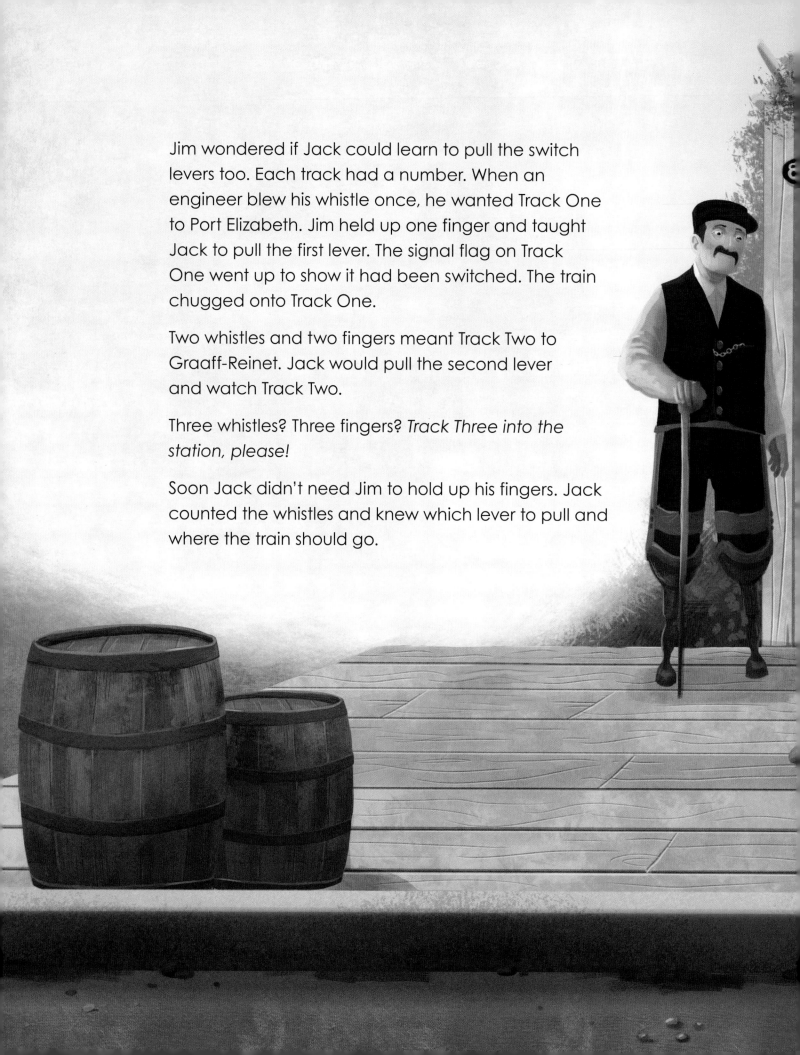

Jim wondered if Jack could learn to pull the switch levers too. Each track had a number. When an engineer blew his whistle once, he wanted Track One to Port Elizabeth. Jim held up one finger and taught Jack to pull the first lever. The signal flag on Track One went up to show it had been switched. The train chugged onto Track One.

Two whistles and two fingers meant Track Two to Graaff-Reinet. Jack would pull the second lever and watch Track Two.

Three whistles? Three fingers? *Track Three into the station, please!*

Soon Jack didn't need Jim to hold up his fingers. Jack counted the whistles and knew which lever to pull and where the train should go.

Some duties were Jim's alone. A monkey simply could not inspect switches, update the log, or operate the telegraph. Even so, Jack was right there, observing. In fact Jack and Jim were rarely apart—except, of course, where baboons weren't allowed. Like railway staff meetings.

"He won't sit still or take turns talking!" said the station master. So Jack had to wait in the hut during meetings.

But Jack didn't like missing out. One night his sad howls drifted from the hut all through the meeting. When Jack was finally let out, he clung to Jim. He squeaked softly while gently touching Jim's face and hands and picking lint off his jacket.

The baboon, however, turned a cold shoulder to the others. Normally the staff enjoyed Jack's trick of shaking hands with them. But when a fellow worker reached out to shake Jack's hand good night, Jack refused to take it. Jack seemed to be blaming him for being left in the hut. Perhaps Jack was waiting for a treat to be offered as an apology.

In the end, Jack extended his hand with an accepting grunt. Then he pushed Jim and the cart off into the darkness toward home.

One day a passenger was horrified to see a baboon pulling levers at the signal hut. She reported it to the railway authorities in Cape Town. They sent a man named Fred Ormsby to investigate.

When Mr. Ormsby saw that a baboon was indeed operating switches and taking the key, Jim was in trouble.

"We can't have a monkey switching the trains! They'll crash!" Mr. Ormsby said.

"Jack can do the work! We'll show you. Please don't fire me. I need this job!" Jim pleaded.

Mr. Ormsby liked Jim and knew his disability brought challenges. He agreed to give Jack a test, but he felt sure a baboon could not pass.

TOOT!

Jack knew what to do. He pulled the lever for Track One. He looked up the tracks and saw the signal flag. He watched the engine shift onto Track One. After it had passed the hut, Jack pushed the lever back into place.

TOOT TOOT!

Jack pulled the lever for Track Two. He looked for the signal and watched where the engine went.

TOOT TOOT TOOT!

Jack switched Track Three.

TOOT TOOT TOOT TOOT!

Upon four whistles, Jack startled Mr. Ormsby when he suddenly sprang away. To the hut he went. He snatched the key, bounded out to the tracks, and held it up for the engineer to take. *Rrrrrr!* The ground shook. *Hisssss!* A cloud of steam swirled. But none of it bothered the hardworking monkey.

Jack had done everything perfectly. Mr. Ormsby was astonished. "How can it be?" he said in disbelief. "He's a *baboon!*"

Not only did Jim keep his job, but the railway hired Jack as Jim's official assistant! They even paid Jack a "wage" of vegetables and fruit.

"Now everyone knows what a special monkey you are," Jim said, stroking Jack's cheek.

The railway authorities discovered that hiring Jack had been a very good decision indeed. People from all over rode trains to the tip of Africa to see the famous baboon at work. As trains passed the hut, passengers greeted Jack and threw snacks to him. This was a game Jack enjoyed almost as much as a cart ride down the hill.

For years Jack and Jim took care of one another. They shared one of the most unusual friendships known between an animal and a human. For nine of those years, Railway Jack, an amazing baboon, switched the rails at Uitenhage Station. It is said that in all that time, he never made a mistake.

AUTHOR'S NOTE

I'm an information nerd. I spend more time than I'd like to admit looking stuff up and reading articles of interest that cross my desk. That's how I stumbled upon a piece about Jack. Intrigued by the extraordinary partnership between Jack and Jim, I set out to learn more. I enjoy the treasure hunt of discovering primary sources to support a story's details. I was able to find accounts by people who'd known the pair. I corresponded with individuals who have materials among personal papers that are not available through other sources. I found local museums that have files on the famous baboon. I located out-of-print books and articles from the archives of bygone newspapers and regional journals. Whenever my sources conflicted, I went with the version I felt was most reliable or suitable for this telling.

What happened to Jack and Jim? In April 1890 Jack died of tuberculosis, a disease that destroys the lungs. Jim nursed Jack to the end as tenderly as a best friend would, and he was quite brokenhearted by the loss. He did not obtain another service animal to replace Jack. Instead, Jim moved back to England, his birth country, and raised a family. Shortly before his own death 30 years later, Jim was interviewed about his experiences with Jack. The interviewer reported that Jim was overcome by emotion as he recalled the animal he'd thought of as a dependable friend. He was a friend who'd given him a mission, enjoyment, and assistance during difficult years; a comrade still missed.

Jack was such an extraordinary representative of his species that Jim hoped there could be an exhibit about him at Albany Museum in Makhanda (formerly Grahamstown), South Africa. Jim's letter to the curator portrayed a touching tribute to Jack when he wrote, "I wish him to be [shown] sitting in a chair with his left hand resting on his knee, as that was a favourite position of his when he was alive." There is still, to this day, a small display at Albany Museum devoted to Jack, the region's most famous baboon.

The old train station where Jack and Jim worked is a museum today as well. An old cart sits silently on the tracks there, waiting to be faithfully pushed home by a devoted, diligent baboon named Jack.

—KT Johnston

"Following investigations by officials, it became evident that Jack was no less skillful and efficient than a trained man, and he was allowed to continue aiding Mr. Wide. In this way, the S.A.R. [South African Railways] officially accepted Jack as an employee, and even provided rations for him thereafter."

— A.J. Havers, Jim Wide's grandson

Jim Wide with Jack, working the levers at their signal hut. The top half of the door is open for easy access to the coal yard key, and the cart can be seen in its usual spot by the platform. (photo taken around 1890)

"RAILWAY JACK."
ASSISTANT POINTSMAN, UITENHAGE STATION. C.P.

(NOT TO BE TAKEN AWAY.

Jack is in position to push the cart and Jim is ready to go. The signal hut and levers are in the background. (photo taken around 1890; from collection of George Howe; used with permission by Euan Nisbet)

Jack is working a lever while Jim observes. It appears the walls inside the hut are papered with train schedules and other clippings. (photo taken around 1890)

A rear view of Uitenhage Station, with trains ready for passengers and freight. (photo taken around 1900)

PRIMATES

Jack was a chacma baboon, the largest of five types of baboons. Chacmas are known for being clever and strong. Baboons are monkeys, and monkeys are primates; so are apes and humans. One way to tell a monkey from an ape is that monkeys have tails. The features that distinguish primates from other mammals are hands with thumbs for grasping, rotating shoulders and hips, large brains, and fingernails.

HISTORY OF SERVICE ANIMALS

* Life was very different for disabled people in the 1880s. Generally, there were no social services to assist them other than family and community. To survive, they had to be self-reliant and creative. They had to do things like build legs and a cart—and recognize the potential help a trained baboon could provide!

* Humans began partnering with animals to help them hunt and alert them to danger at least 15,000 years ago.

* Archaeologists have found 2,000-year-old drawings showing blind people using dogs as guides.

* Paintings and other evidence of guide dogs and comfort animals became more common during the 1700s and 1800s.

* The modern concept of formally trained guide dogs originated in Germany after World War I. This was a result of the thousands of returning soldiers who had been blinded by poisonous gas.

* The first seeing-eye dog in the United States was imported from a training center in Switzerland in 1928—about 45 years after Jim trained Jack the baboon to assist him.

* It wasn't until the mid–1900s that animals were recognized as providing more than sight guidance. Today some animals are trained to bring attention to medical issues, some perform tasks like Jack did, and some provide emotional comfort to individuals with disability-related stress.

* Dogs were initially the service animal of choice because of their dedication to humans, trainability, and the things they could be taught to do. Today many different species provide assistance.

GLOSSARY

amputate—to surgically remove a damaged limb, such as a finger or leg

engineer—a person who operates a train

railway—an international term for *railroad*

signal—a device along the tracks that provides instruction to the engineer such as to stop or proceed, or which track the train will travel on

signalman—a person who sets the switches to move trains to a different track; a signal flag lets the engineer know the tracks are set correctly

switch—a movable mechanism built into the tracks that opens or closes to allow a train to stay on one track or move to another track

wage—payment for work done

DISCUSSION QUESTIONS

* Look at the photos of Jack. In what ways did he seem human? What do you think makes humans different from other animals?

* Have you ever seen a service animal working? What was it doing to assist its human?

* Some people might say Jim took advantage of Jack, and that a baboon should be left in the wild. Do you agree or disagree with that idea, and why?

* What might have happened to Jim if he hadn't had Jack in his life?

* If you were going to look up more information about this story at the library or on the internet, what keywords would you use in your search?

INTERNET RESOURCES

* *How a switch changes where a train goes:*
  https://www.youtube.com/embed/3NELFCMl3co?autoplay=1&start=21&end=67&rel=0

* *How levers control the switches:*
  https://www.youtube.com/embed/ZuR5QTlfOzk?autoplay=1&start=304&end=318&rel=0

* *How a steam engine works:*
  https://www.youtube.com/embed/g8LrAsL4oH0?autoplay=1&start=29&end=92&rel=0

* *More about Jack and Jim:*
  http://www.history101.com/signalman-jack-the-baboon-railroad-worker/

* *Learn about the different types of assistance animals:*
  http://www.animalplanet.com/difference-between-service-therapy-support-dogs/

* *Discover some unusual species of assistance animals:*
  https://www.youtube.com/embed/QpatXVnxJll?autoplay=1&end=470&rel=0

READ MORE

Applegate, Katherine, and G. Brian Karas. *Ivan: The Remarkable True Story of the Shopping Mall Gorilla*. Boston: Clarion Books, 2014.

Hoena, Blake A. *Stubby the Dog Soldier: World War I Hero*. North Mankato, MN: Picture Window Books, 2015.

McCully, Emily Arnold. *Clara: The (Mostly) True Story of the Rhinoceros Who Dazzled Kings, Inspired Artists, and Won the Hearts of Everyone . . . While She Ate Her Way Up and Down a Continent!* New York: Schwartz & Wade Books, 2016.

Newman, Lesléa, and Amy June Bates. *Ketzel, the Cat Who Composed*. Somerville, MA: Candlewick Press, 2015.

BIBLIOGRAPHY

Barritt, David, "Baboon Was Once Railway Signalman," *People Magazine South Africa*, July 21, 1987.

Eshak, Boeti, "Legend Grows about Baboon Jack on the Old Cape Railway," *The Sunday Times*, November 11, 1990.

Fitzsimons, F. W. "Mammals, Volume 1." *The Natural History of South Africa*. London: Longmans, Green and Co., 1919, pp. 61–64.

Havers, A. J., "Jack the Signalman," *The Cape Argus*, October 18, 1947.

Havers, A. J., "Where Will It Stop?" *The Nongqai*, December 1947.

Howe, George B., "A Unique Signalman," *The Railway Signal 8*, no. 9, 1890, p. 185.

Lobjoit, C. W., "Monkey Business: An Old Story Authenticated," *South African Railways and Harbours Magazine*, Vol. 1 No. 8, August 1948.

Moorman, "A Novel Signalman," *Illustrated Sporting and Dramatic News*, March 29, 1890, quoted in "An Odd Signalman," *Clinch Valley News*, August 1, 1890.

Sellick, W. S. J. *Uitenhage, Past and Present*. Uitenhage, Eastern Cape, South Africa: Uitenhage Times, 1904.

Webster, Roger. "The Baboon of Uitenhage." *At the Fireside: True South African Stories*, Volume 3, pp. 29–30. Cape Town, South Africa: New Africa Books, 2005.

For our animal friends, who take our hearts and give their all,
in service and devotion—KT Johnston

AUTHOR ACKNOWLEDGMENTS

I am profoundly grateful to my editor, Kristen Mohn, and the rest of the team at Capstone for falling in love with Jack and helping me tell his story. Infinite appreciation goes to Jonathan and Nan, my cheerleaders extraordinaire and honest critics—without whom this book would not have materialized. Any accomplishment starts with inspiration, and coffee chats with these dear friends created the spark. I also wish to thank Dr. Euan Nisbet for kindly sharing his great-great uncle George Howe's papers; Mr. Denis Murphy for supplying information from his personal collection; and Port Elizabeth Museum at Bayworld, Albany History Museum, National Library of South Africa, and The British Library for providing material from their archives.

ABOUT THE AUTHOR

KT Johnston found history a boring subject in school—but now it's the passion of her writing. She earned a degree in biology and conducted animal behavior studies before switching to a corporate career. After raising two children and several litters of curly-coated retrievers, KT began writing, spotlighting special animals who had affected the lives of everyday people. She and her husband live in Minneapolis where the four-legged members of their family have always been special. KT hopes to inspire others to be curious about our world, one true story at a time.

ABOUT THE ILLUSTRATOR

César Samaniego was born in Barcelona, Spain, in 1975. He grew up with an artist father, smelling his father's oils, reading his comic books, and trying to paint over his father's illustrations! He attended Llotja Arts and Crafts School and graduated with honors in 2010. Since then he has published many books and provided art for apps, textbooks, and animations. César lives in Canet de Mar, a small coastal town near Barcelona, with his wife, daughter, five cats, and a crazy dog.

Railway Jack is published by Capstone Editions, an imprint of Capstone.
1710 Roe Crest Drive, North Mankato, Minnesota 56003
www.capstonepub.com

Text copyright © 2020 by KT Johnston
Illustration copyright © 2020 by Capstone

Library of Congress Cataloging-in-Publication Data is available on the Library of Congress website.
ISBN: 978-1-68446-088-5 (hardcover)
ISBN: 978-1-68446-089-2 (ebook PDF)

Editorial Credits
Kristen Mohn, editor; Lori Bye and Kay Fraser, designers; Svetlana Zhurkin, media researcher; Katy LaVigne, production specialist

Image Credits
Alamy: FLHC A20, 35 (bottom), History and Art Collection, 35 (top); Courtesy of Euan Nisbet/Papers of Rev. George Howe and Martha Storr Osborn-Howe, 34; Shutterstock: Benny Marty, 36 (bottom), Zuzana Gabrielov, 36 (top); Wikimedia, 33

All internet sites appearing in back matter were available and accurate when this book was sent to press.